GUIDE TO

CENTRAL SECTOR

of

HADRIAN'S WALL

by

Robin Birley, M.A., F.S.A.

NORTHERN HISTORY BOOKLET No. 19

Published by

Frank Graham, 6 Queen's Terrace, Newcastle upon Tyne NE2 2PL

For Daphne and Pat

First Published 1972

SBN 902833 456

Printed by
J. W. Moore Limited, North Shields

CONTENTS

PREFACE

THIS GUIDE BOOK is designed to help the visitor find his way round the outstanding remains of the Wall. If it stimulates him to read more deeply about the subject, it will have served its purpose.

A one inch O.S. map is as invaluable an aid here as anywhere else, and it will help to overcome the somewhat vague signposting. Much of the Wall runs through hilly countryside, where casual footwear is not advised.

Any work on the Wall owes much to a long line of scholars, past and present, and I beg their indulgence if I have misrepresented their research. Fortunately there is still much controversy about the facts, and we still have a long way to go before some answers are possible.

INTRODUCTION

HADRIAN'S WALL has been described as the outstanding ancient monument north of the Alps, and it has fascinated both generations of scholars and tens of thousands of ordinary people who annually wander among its ruins and ponder for a while the departed glory of Rome. Its fascination lies in the many sides of its character and in its magnificent situation: some see it as a great engineering feat, some feel sorry for the soldiers who once manned its forts and milecastles; others perhaps secretly see it as the forgotten answer to the Scots – or thankfully compare its ruinous state with other more efficient Walls elsewhere. It has attracted a considerable volume of erroneous myths; chariots driving along the Wall, speaking trumpets built into the Wall, lonely Italian soldiers mournfully gazing through the freezing fog at hairy Picts about to assault the battlements – but it has also attracted a vast library of serious academic literature. Knowledge of the Wall's history has advanced considerably in the past seventy years or so, but there is a great deal more to be learned. Hadrian's Wall is so familiar to British children that people sometimes think of it as having told us all that we can possibly hope to know about its history, but the fact remains that little more than 1 % of its structures have yet been examined scientifically by archaeologists. Many of its forts and towns are buried beneath modern cities, and a long stretch of the Wall itself is now covered with the tarmac of the Military Road, between Newcastle and Chollerford, but as much again lies beneath green fields, safe for the moment from further destruction.

The visitor to the Wall should remember that much more has been examined by archaeologists than is now preserved for his inspection. Excavation is a costly business, but the treatment of the exposed buildings and their display as an ancient monument costs a great deal more. Landowners are sometimes prepared to allow parts of their property to be excavated, but they often do not relish the prospect of visitors coming to see the remains, and excavation is usually allowed only if the land is restored to its former condition afterwards. Even if they are prepared to give some of their property to the nation, the Department of the Environment, who usually deal with the conservation and display of ancient monuments, are not always able to accept the gift.

Many people feel that the remains of Hadrian's Wall, like other major monuments, are part of the national heritage and should belong to the nation. The facts of the matter are that a part of the national heritage they undoubtedly are, but the land on which they stand usually belongs to a private individual who has to earn his living from it. There are parts of Hadrian's Wall where visitors are not welcome, and other areas where local farmers would dearly like to see visitors excluded. This hostile attitude is not new, but it has come to the fore with the great increase in the number of people who visit the remains since the last war. The fault lies on both sides: some visitors do not obey the country code and the stupid behaviour of the few casts a shadow over the majority. By the same token, if the public footpaths were better marked and more information available, fewer visitors would stray into hayfields and attempt to climb old field walls. Visitors must remember, therefore, that the monuments to be described in this book lie in the heart of the Northumbrian countryside, and they must do their best to observe the sensible country code: don't climb the field walls, use the gates; don't leave litter about the place; and above all keep the dog on a lead.

The Sources

Our knowledge of the Wall is built up from many widely different sources, and since fresh information is often coming to light, it is impossible to write a history of its life that will not need considerable modification within a few years. This is a very healthy situation. Many vital points are still the subject of intense academic enquiry and will not be entered into here, but the visitor should know something of the differing sources which are drawn upon by the historian of the Wall.

Classical authors tell us very little – there are conflicting claims for both Hadrian and Severus as the builders – and Roman army documents only give some indication of the names and garrison of the forts. But epigraphy (the study of inscribed stones, etc.) fills in many serious gaps in our knowledge, and the majority of all the Roman inscriptions found in Britain come from this Northern Frontier. A knowledge of other Roman frontiers sometimes adds to our knowledge, for the Roman army was very methodical, and its organisation on the Danube, for example, will not have differed much from its organisation in Britain. Archaeology obviously makes the highest contribution to our knowledge, and it should be remembered that today archaeology is much more than just digging for relics of the past: the skills of a wide variety of specialists, varying from the botanist to the numismatist, are available to the excavator, and it is not unusual for over a dozen such specialists to be participating in the examination of evidence from a site. Finally, the historical record would be very lean without the contributions of many acute observers in the past: men and women who saw the remains before they were so drastically robbed of their stone or levelled for modern building sites and roads. This northern frontier has been fortunate in its impressive roll of antiquarians, from Bede to Camden, Horsley, Hodgson and a host of others. There is still much to be learnt from a study of their pages.

The remains

It is sad to recall that most of what the visitor will see when he visits the Wall, both structures and finds, were excavated a long time ago. Chesters was excavated by its owner, John Clayton,

6

from 1843 onwards – he owned Carrawburgh, Housesteads, Vindolanda and Carvoran at one time, and his influence prevented much destruction; Housesteads was largely examined between 1898 and 1899 by R. C. Bosanquet, and Corbridge 1906-1914. But the Durham University Excavation Committee has been responsible for much important work since then, although not all of it can be seen today, and the formation of the Vindolanda Trust in 1970 has given fresh impetus to the work at both Vindolanda and Carvoran.

This guide is concerned only with the principal remains in the most spectacular stretch of the Wall, between Corbridge and Birdoswald, where most visitors receive their introduction to Roman frontier studies. There are, however, notable places outside this area which are well worth a visit. In Carlisle, the Tullie House Museum has a fine collection of Roman stones and small finds from the Cumberland area, and in the east, the Museum of Antiquities at Newcastle University is an outstanding Museum, devoted to material from the earliest appearance of man to 1066, and containing both impressive Roman objects and informative models, together with the reconstructed temple to Mithras. The visitor who penetrates as far as South Shields will find some of the remains of the fort there laid out in a park, together with a small Museum, whilst at Benwell, on the outskirts of Newcastle, the temple of Antenociticus and the Vallum crossing look rather uncomfortable amongst the brick buildings of the modern day.

A select bibliography is included at the end of this book for those who wish to explore the area in greater depth, or to study for themselves the excavation reports and the antiquarian accounts of individual sites.

HISTORICAL OUTLINE

Roman patrols had probably penetrated to the Tyne-Solway gap before A.D. 71, when Brigantia was invaded, but the earliest forts date to the time of the governor Agricola, A.D. 78-84. At that time the Romans aimed at the total conquest of the island, but the Highlands of Scotland and their intransigent inhabitants proved too much for them. Other campaigns on the Continent demanded reinforcement from the troops in Britain, and by A.D. 100 the army had retired to the Stanegate line. This frontier was based upon the road running between Carlisle, Corbridge and South Shields, with large forts at seven mile intervals – Carvoran, Vindolanda, Newbrough and Corbridge were probably part of this system.

A series of disturbances in the north demonstrated that this frontier was inefficient, and Hadrian (A.D. 117-138), with several alternatives open to him, ordered the construction of the great Wall which bears his name. The exact date for the commencement of construction and details of the various changes of plan are still a matter for dispute, but some now feel that work began in A.D. 120 on the first plan, involving a ten foot wide wall from Newcastle to the Irthing, and a turf wall from there to Bowness on Solway, with milecastles and turrets at regular intervals along the line. At this stage, the main garrison remained in their Stanegate forts, now perhaps reinforced by more troops. Hadrian visited Britain for the only time in his career in A.D. 122, and perhaps it was then that the first plan was abandoned in favour of a much more ambitious and expensive scheme. This second plan lengthened the Wall by extending it to Wallsend in the east, moved the garrison forward to forts attached to the Wall, and placed the broad ditch with ramparts on either berm (the Vallum) to the south of the complex, creating a military zone secure from surprise attack. At what stage the continuation of the milecastles, turrets and forts down the Cumberland coast from Bowness to St. Bees Head was planned is not known for certain – perhaps it was a part of the original scheme. There were in addition three outpost forts north of the Wall in the western sector (Birrens, Netherby and Bewcastle). The considerable additional burden of construction was alleviated by the arrival of the Sixth legion (Victrix) from Germany, and by a reduction in the thickness of the Wall in sectors where it had not yet been completed. By circa A.D. 128 the new frontier was in commission.

Hadrian's biographer states that the Wall was built to separate the Romans from the barbarians, but the truth was probably more complex. There were numerous untamed people to the south of the Tyne-Solway gap, and the Wall at least rendered their union with other enemies to the north more difficult. The Wall also demonstrated to all the local inhabitants that Rome's authority could only be questioned by a show of force that was probably beyond their means, and it was to serve as a very efficient customs and police barrier. It was also the personal solution of a very unusual emperor, a man of considerable intelligence who loved to dabble in architecture. Whatever its purpose, the Wall was not designed for a fighting platform, for the Roman army was never trained or equipped to fight from such an undignified position.

A study of the forts along the Wall indicates that at either end there were strong cavalry forces, with the central forts being manned by part-mounted infantry. There were also, of course, many forts to the south of the Wall, spread out in the Pennines, guarding roads and important river crossings. Overall command of this new frontier lay with the legionary general at York, but local command would have been exercised by the commanding officer of the double strength cavalry regiment at Stanwix, to the north of the river Eden from Carlisle.**

*NOTE: Milecastles and turrets have been numbered, the series beginning in the east. The turrets take the number of the preceding milecastle to the east, with the letters 'a' and 'b' to indicate the first and second turret. A Roman mile is generally reckoned to have been 1,618 yards, and the turrets should thus be nearly 540 yards apart. The majority of both milecastles and turrets lie close to the theoretical position.

After the death of Hadrian (A.D. 138), his successor Antoninus Pius authorised a fresh advance into Scotland, where a Turf Wall was constructed between Forth and Clyde. Hadrian's Wall was probably maintained by skeleton forces, with most of its installations boarded up. The history of the years between A.D. 140 and 211 is far from certain: there were at least two periods of occupation on the Antonine Wall separated by a time of disuse, and both Walls appear to have been extensively damaged by the uprising of A.D. 197, when much of the army was absent in Gaul during governor Albinus' vain attempt to seize the imperial throne from Severus. Severus ordered major reconstruction of Hadrian's Wall before coming to Britain in person, with a large force, to crush Maeatae and Caledonians, those responsible for the damage. Judging by his fort buildings in Scotland he intended to occupy the whole country, but his death at York in A.D. 211 allowed other counsels to prevail, and his son Caracalla withdrew the army once more to Hadrian's Wall.

From A.D. 211 onwards, Hadrian's Wall was the effective frontier of Roman Britain. It was not, however, a frontier in the modern sense of a hard and fast line dividing two sovereign territories: there were several large forts to the north of the Wall in the lands of tribes who had probably entered into some form of treaty relationship with Rome. Their loyalty would be reinforced by cavalry patrols and the benefits of advantageous trading terms.

The remainder of the third century appears to have been one of some prosperity on the frontier, as considerable civilian settlements grew up outside the forts. Political troubles in A.D. 296, similar to those of A.D. 197, had the same effect, and Constantius Chlorus had to carry out a considerable rebuilding programme, in A.D. 300. The fourth century saw the gradual decline in status of the auxiliary regiments stationed on the Wall as both internal and external pressures bore down upon the Roman Empire. Sea-borne raids saw the creation of more advanced armies, and the real military power lay with the new field groups, dominated by heavily-armed cavalry. Lack of interest by the central government affected pay and probably recruitment as well, and when the most serious assault of all concerned, in A.D. 367 (the 'barbarian conspiracy'), the Wall was overrun – as was most of Britain. Energetic action by Count Theodosius, Valentinian's fierce general, restored order once more, and many Wall forts were rebuilt, but in a cruder style than before. The garrisons had been reinforced or replaced by fresh levies who did not have the same traditions behind them, although their building style demonstrates considerable energy.

It is difficult to envisage the last years of the Wall. Successive troops withdrawals between A.D. 383 and 410 undoubtedly drained away most of the effective military strength, but people undoubtedly continued to live in some of the forts and towns along the line of the Wall. They may now have come under the control of the sub-Roman kingdoms of the north – Rheged, Strathclyde and Manau Goddodin – and played their part in the continuing struggle against Picts and overseas invaders. There are strong Arthurian legends in both west Northumberland and in Cumberland, and some see Camboglanna (Birdoswald) as Arthur's Camelot. But that is another story.

THE ARMY OF OCCUPATION

The forts along the frontier were occupied by infantry battalions and cavalry regiments in the main, drawn from the very large military forces which the Roman government was forced to maintain in Britain. It was a cosmopolitan force drawn from all the corners of the Empire, and with few men from Italy in its ranks. It was welded together into a coherent whole by its traditions of discipline and thorough training, backed up by the unifying force of a common official language and paymaster, and by a degree of common religious faith.

The backbone of this army, and the most highly skilled and paid men, were to be found in the legions. There were usually about 30 of these army groups in the Empire at any given time, each with a nominal roll of 6,000 men, all Roman citizens in the second century (unlike the soldiers in the auxiliary regiments). For most of the life of Hadrian's Wall, there were three legions serving in Britain: the most recently arrived was the Sixth Victrix, which came over in A.D. 122 to reinforce the construction gangs on the Wall and subsequently moved into the Ninth legion's base at York, command headquarters of the northern military zone; the Twentieth Valeria Victrix, stationed at Chester, and the Second Augusta from Caerleon in south Wales also played a major part in the construction of the Wall. Whether or not the Ninth Legion was still in Britain at this time is not known.

Evidence of legionary troops serving on Hadrian's Wall has been found, but the circumstances are normally exceptional. They built the structures and then retired to their own comfortable fortresses further south: emergencies brought them back from time to time, and for much of the third century there were small detachments from two legions permanently stationed at Corbridge, presumably craftsmen engaged in armaments work.

As far as the natives of the north were concerned, their contact with Rome and its civilisation came in the main from the auxiliary troops, many of whom were not Roman citizens in the second century. The regiments had been originally from tribal groups, often under the command of their own chieftains; their titles often give a clue to their history. When they came to Britain they might still contain largely troops from their country of origin, but local recruitment when stationed in foreign parts meant that a regiment of Gauls, for example, did not necessarily contain men drawn from that country. By the third and fourth centuries, most of the soldiers had probably been born in Britain, often in the settlements outside the walls of forts. The regiments probably retained their distinctive uniforms or weapon specialities, and tradition undoubtedly ensured the survival of special customs. The commanding officers of these regiments were drawn from the equestrian ranks of Roman citizens, and usually spent three or four years in the command before moving to another post, either in the army or in civilian administration.

There were several categories of auxiliary units. In descending order of seniority and pay, they were the milliary *ala* (1,000 strong cavalry regiment – there was only one in Britain, and it was stationed at Stanwix, near Carlisle, which was thus the headquarters of the Wall command), the 500 strong *ala* (cavalry), the 1,000 strong part-mounted infantry battalion, the 500 strong part-mounted infantry battalion, and the 1,000 strong and 500 strong infantry battalions. In addition, there were some specialist regiments, such as archers. By the beginning of the third century, units known as *numeri* are attested in Britain. These apparently varied in strength between 200 and 800 men, and were drawn from the outermost borders of the Empire, a good deal less disciplined and civilised than their auxiliary colleagues. In the third century, for example, the *numerus Hnaudifridi* appears to have been brigaded with the perhaps below-strength battalion of Tungrians at Housesteads.

There was also, of course, the fleet, whose men are recorded as having built part of Benwell fort, but their task was normally that of bringing up the military stores to the ports on east and west coasts.

It was an extraordinarily cosmopolitan force that was stationed for so long on this northern frontier of the Roman Empire: at one time or another there were Syrian archers at Carvoran, Moors at Burgh-by-Sands, Tigris boatmen at South Shields, a British regiment at Newcastle upon Tyne, Gauls at Vindolanda, Tungrians at Housesteads, Asturian horsemen from Spain at Chesters – and so on. Constant intermarriage with the local women must in time have produced one of the most inter-mixed populations in Europe. Perhaps it is from this that the modern Northumbrian draws his strength.

GARRISON LIFE ON THE FRONTIER

Some visitors think of both Hadrian's Wall and its forts as being under constant attack from a mixture of Picts and Scots. Whilst there must have been disturbed periods and occasional onslaughts, the normal routine of the Roman army regiments on the Wall was designed to keep up military morale and discipline in the face of an army's worst enemy, long periods of peace. Most armies, since the creation of permanent standing forces, have wrestled with this problem with mixed success, and the Romans were as successful as anyone.

In the first place, it is salutory to remember that the Roman army was not trained to fight from a static position: the impressive fort walls and ditches were designed to enable a skeleton force to hold the base in safety whilst the major part of the garrison was engaged elsewhere. When danger threatened, the army marched out to meet it in the open, where its carefully rehearsed battle formations and manoeuvring could be relied upon to scatter less disciplined forces.

The normal daily routine of the Wall regiments fell into several clear compartments. There was guard duty and the numerous parades and documentation essential to a sophisticated army; weapon training, drill and physical fitness was an everyday chore; fatigues – cleaning and polishing, fetching stores, bringing in firewood, mucking out stables, repairing broken equipment – were time-consuming and boring, but essential; food had to be prepared and eaten. Above all, there were frequent route marches and mock battles, for Josephus has pointed out that these were the secret of Rome's long military success – the 'bloodless battles' were so effective that real warfare was no more than 'bloody manoeuvres'.

Alongside the normal routine there would be diversions. Reconnaissance patrols would have to be organised, and there was always the chance of getting out of the fort for a few days as guard to a stores convoy. Regimental holidays, on the Emperor's birthday or some notable anniversary, would ensure a day off, after a parade and religious observances. Sometimes major engineering projects would take up months at a time, as new roads were constructed or the fort walls rebuilt. It would have been a tedious life if there had been no civilian population nearby, but many of the soldiers were married – or in the second century had established permanent liaisons with women in the face of a legal ban on marriage – and there were shops and inns outside the forts, as well as the military bath-house, the Roman equivalent of the NAAFI.

There is no doubt that men from Syria or the Tigris might find life in the north of Britain uncongenial, but to those from western Europe it was perfectly tolerable, and many of the troops must have been born locally. The myth of unbearable northern winters which still finds currency in the south of England is laughable to those who actually lived – or still live – up here.

CIVILIANS ON THE FRONTIER

Sixty years ago the existence of civilian settlements outside the forts in the north was virtually unknown, although general knowledge of what usually happens when an army settles down in a foreign land should have prepared historians to search for them. Since then, aerial photography in particular has shown the large extent of the settlements: both Carlisle and Corbridge were walled towns of nearly 70 and 30 acres respectively, whilst the forts in this area all have substantial buildings outside them, usually covering many more acres than the fort itself. The impact of these civilians must have been very great: army morale and recruitment would be vitally affected, but so too would the entire social and economic life of the region.

Only at Housesteads and Vindolanda can the visitor now see something of these small frontier towns where the wives and children, the merchants and craftsmen, the priests and slaves lived. But it is worth looking at them closely, for a diet of nothing but military installations gives a very unbalanced picture of the Roman frontier.

A building inscription from Birdoswald, recording reconstruction of a building under the governor Modius Julius (A.D. 219).

Within a few years the entire settlement outside the fort of Vindolanda should have been excavated, and historians will be in a position to analyse the evidence of standards of living, occupations and degree of Romanisation. But it is already clear that the *vicani Vindolandesses*, as they called themselves on an altar found in 1914 (now in Chesters Museum), were far removed from the traditional view of civilians on the frontier – native squatters. Indeed, in the third and fourth centuries there is no reason to believe that the civilians were very different, either racially or materially, from the soldiers inside the forts. Intermarriage and the benefits of trade had made a big impact.

Some buildings outside the forts are military, for the bath-house and many of the temples would rarely be constructed inside the fort itself, and spaces must have been reserved for a transport park, hay-stacks and fuel.

13

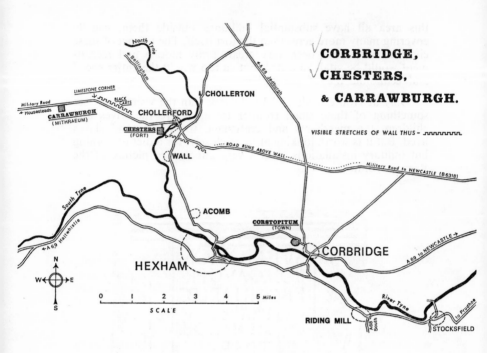

CORBRIDGE,
CHESTERS,
& CARRAWBURGH.

VISIBLE STRETCHES OF WALL THUS- ᴧᴧᴧᴧᴧᴧᴧᴧ.

11 inches by 6 inches.

PED[ATVRA] CLA[SSIS]
BRI[TANNICAE.]

The length (built by)
the British Fleet.

Ɔ FLORINI
P[ASSVS] XXII

The century of Florinus
[built] twenty-two paces.

14

CORBRIDGE (CORSTOPITUM)

Opening hours		Weekdays	Sundays
	Mar. – April	9.30 – 5.30	2.00 – 5.30
	May – Sept.	9.30 – 7.00	9.30 – 7.00
	October	9.30 – 5.30	2.00 – 5.30
	Nov. – Feb.	9.30 – 4.00	2.00 – 4.00

Admission   Adults 7½p; Children (under 15) 4p.
Reduced rates for parties.

Car park in the heart of the site.

Museum. Custodian. Guide-book by Eric Birley, other literature, replicas, slides, postcards, etc.

Visible remains: Two granaries, town fountain and water-tank, enigmatic site XI (?storehouse, ?Forum, ?Legionary Headquarters), fragmentary walling of legionary compounds, miniature headquarters building and a variety of ill-preserved houses and temples.

Corstopitum was one of the most important Roman sites in the north, and it developed into the second town of the frontier region (Carlisle was the largest). Here the main trunk road from the south (Dere Street or Watling Street) crossed the Tyne on a bridge before sweeping north into modern Scotland: to the south of the bridge it probably met the branch road which led to Whitley Castle near Alston, the centre of Roman lead working, and to the north of the bridge, in the middle of the site, it crossed the Stanegate, the principal east-west trunk road.

There were at least three timber forts here before Hadrian's Wall was built, when Corstopitum was one of the Stanegate frontier forts. When Scotland was re-occupied in A.D. 140, it became an important staging post for troops or military stores in transit. Later it became a depot for legionary craftsmen, and a substantial walled town grew up around the legionary compounds. Occupation continued into the fifth century.

Only a fraction of the known remains can now be seen in the area which was placed in the guardianship of the Department of the Environment by the owner, the late David Cuthbert. Most of the buildings were excavated between 1906 and 1914, but the Durham University Excavation Committee has been examining the earlier structures which lie below since 1935. Much of Hexham Abbey and Corbridge parish church was carted away from this Roman town, which can claim the dubious honour of the oldest recorded excavation in Britain – King John set his troops to

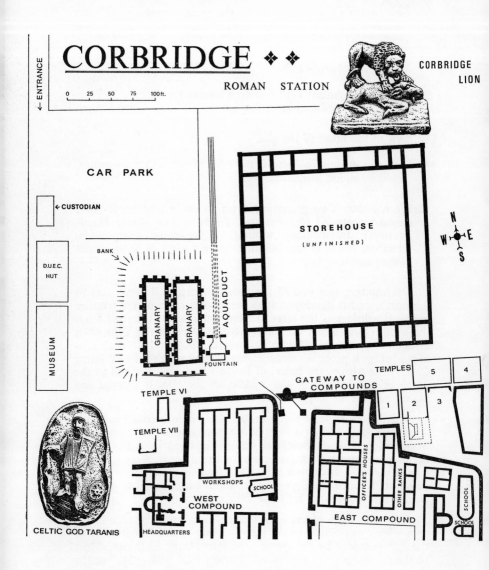

CORBRIDGE ❖ ❖

ROMAN STATION

CORBRIDGE LION

0 25 50 75 100 ft.

← ENTRANCE

CAR PARK

← CUSTODIAN

D.U.E.C. HUT

MUSEUM

BANK

GRANARY

GRANARY

AQUADUCT

FOUNTAIN

STOREHOUSE

(UNFINISHED)

N
W E
S

TEMPLES

5 4

1 2 3

GATEWAY TO COMPOUNDS

TEMPLE VI

TEMPLE VII

WORKSHOPS

SCHOOL

WEST COMPOUND

HEADQUARTERS

OFFICER'S HOUSES

OTHER RANKS

EAST COMPOUND

SCHOOL

SCHOOL

CELTIC GOD TARANIS

Housesteads fort from the south-east. The fort lies uneasily on the slope of the Whin Sill ridge, and the *vicus* or frontier town grew up to the south and east of the fort walls.

Crag Lough and the Whin Sill, from above Hot Bank farm to the east. Although the Wall is no longer visible on these crags, it is the most popular section of the frontier, with magnificent views in all directions.

The Wall ditch running down the eastern slopes of Winshields Crags, the highest part of the frontier: Steel Rigg car-park lies amongst the trees in the middle distance.

The Whin Sill and Vallum, looking east towards Winshields, where the Wall was forced to twist and turn on the summit of the crags, the Vallum took the direct line whenever possible. Although it was in no sense a military defensive barrier, the Vallum effectively protected the stores and cattle belonging to the Wall regiments.

Column bases at Corbridge, the second largest town on the frontier, and the base of legionary craftsmen. Buildings here were on a grander scale than elsewhere, reflecting the importance of its economic life.

The Wall above Walltown quarry. This is probably the most instructive section of the Wall now visible, and the views in all directions are superb. Near here can be found chives and other herbs, perhaps first introduced to the area by Roman troops.

Chesters Military bath-house, from the south bank of the North Tyne, close to the bridge abutment. This is probably the best preserved Roman building in the North of England.

The temple to MITHRAS at Carrawburgh, outside the south-west angle of the fort. The shrine to *Coventina* lies to the north-west, by the field wall.

This magnificent silver dish was found on the bank of the Tyne below the modern bridge in 1734. How it found its way there is a mystery, for it must have belonged to a wealthy officer. It is thought to have been made in the late fourth century.

work here in 1201, looking for treasure. He found none, but the excavators before World War One found a bronze jug with 160 gold coins in it, the largest hoard of Roman gold ever found in Britain. Replicas of these coins could once be seen in the Museum – the originals are in the British Museum.

The Museum. The ramshackle and undistinguished looking building which houses the display of objects found on the site should not deter the visitor from a close inspection of the contents. Here one will see some fine inscriptions or sculptured stones, together with a historically valuable collection of small finds – the surgeon's instruments and the blacksmith's tools are most revealing. The objects deserve a better home, but the Trustees who administer this Museum do not have access to the admission money which visitors pay for entrance – the same applies at Chesters and Housesteads.

To the untrained eye, the southern half of the site is a jumble of fragmentary walls of different periods. It is best to concentrate on the northern half at first. The massive granaries, with their loading bays, buttresses and heavy flagged floors are the best of their kind to be seen on the frontier, whilst the remains of the fountain with its aqueduct near by hint at a splendour not found on the other Wall sites. The most remarkable building on the frontier lies to the east, the vast site XI, variously interpreted as a storehouse, a projected Forum and a projected legionary headquarters building. Whatever its destined purpose, it was never completed, and smaller structures, mostly removed in modern times, were later built on its acre of ground. Its masonry is exceptionally fine.

To the south of the road lie the legionary compounds: the most intelligible structure is the miniature headquarters building in the south-west corner, which has a fine sunken strongroom.

✓ CHESTERS (CILURNUM)

		Weekdays	Sundays
Opening hours	March – April	9.00 – 5.00	2.00 – 4.30
	May – Sept.	9.00 – 5.30	2.00 – 5.00
	Oct. – Feb.	9.30 – 4.00	2.00 – 4.00
Admission	Adults 7½p; Children (under 15) 4p. Special rates for parties.		

Museum. *Car-park* close to site. *Cafe.*

The remains are in the guardianship of the Department of the Environment.

Guide-book by Eric Birley; Postcards, etc.

Visible remains: Very fine military bath-house, headquarters building, part of commanding officer's house, portions of barrack buildings, five of the six gateways, four wall turrets and short stretches of fort wall. Across the river (North Tyne), part of the eastern bridge abutment.

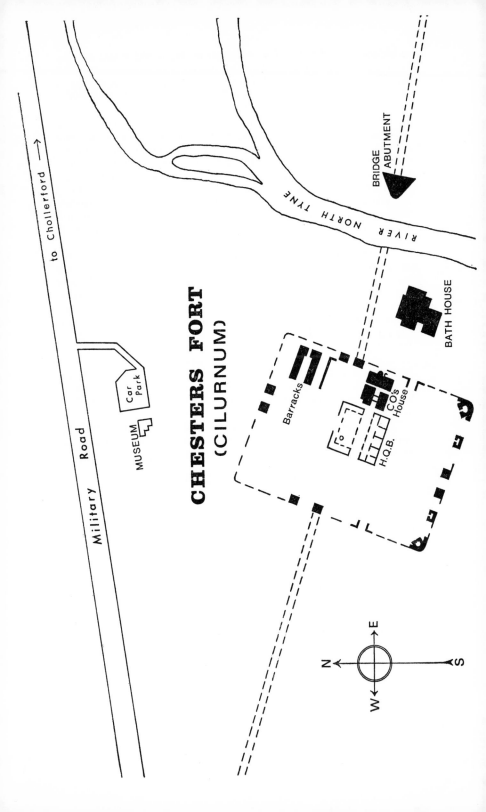

CHESTERS FORT
(CILURNUM)

to Chollerford →

Military Road

MUSEUM

Car Park

RIVER NORTH TYNE

BRIDGE ABUTMENT

BATH HOUSE

Barracks

CO's House

H.Q.B.

N W E S

Area of fort:	5¾ acres. *Large vicus or town*, mainly to the south.

Garrison	Second century:	*a.* cavalry regiment.
		b. First cohort of Dalmatians
	Third and fourth centuries:	Second ala of Asturians

Chesters is generally reckoned to have been the most picturesque and desirable posting on the wall, and its remains are well preserved. If archaeologists were allowed to complete the work of John Clayton in the nineteenth century, this would be a monument without parallel in Britain.

The Museum contains the finest collection of inscribed stones to be found in the north, for John Clayton, a former owner of the large house near by, once owned Carrawburgh, Housesteads, Vindolanda and Carvoran as well. Here the visitor will find the material from Coventina's Well at Carrawburgh, and the very rare Carvoran *modius*, a bronze corn-measure. Amongst the inscribed stones, the rarest are the great altar or inscribed pillar from the shrine of Mars Thincsus at Housesteads (it dominates the packed ranks of the altars), and the fragmentary tombstone of Brigomaglos, a fifth century Christian who died at Vindolanda (it is on a shelf near the door).

Dedication slab from Chesters, recording reconstruction of a building in the reign of Elagabalus. A.D. 221

Behind the table to the right of the door is the important Vindolanda altar – a dedication to the god of smiths, Vulcan, set up by the '*vicani Vindolandesses*', the civilians of Vindolanda. The visitor may see the small collection box for donations towards the costs of this Museum: the Trustees who administer it do not have access to the admission money paid at the gate, and this fine collection of Roman material deserves a better display than it receives at the moment.

As the visitor walks across the field to the fort, he will appreciate the wonderful situation of this site. There is nothing particularly remarkable about the fort defences, but only here can one see how a cavalry fort was constructed across the Wall, with six gateways. The Headquarters building is much more ornate than those at Housesteads and Vindolanda, for the garrison here was a cavalry regiment, with higher status and pay. The sunken strongroom in the eastern range of administrative rooms is well preserved – when first excavated its iron-studded door was still in position.

The commanding officer's house is only partially excavated, but there is a good example of Roman hypocaust heating, whilst the barrack buildings, equally fragmentary, are nevertheless standing quite high, and show how they lay together in pairs, with the officer's flat protruding at one end of each building.

The outstanding building here is the military bath-house down by the river. There are small notices in most rooms explaining their function, but the visitor should remember that the building was altered several times in Roman days. These bath-houses served as a combination between a turkish bath and the troops' NAAFI, where they could relax in comfort at the end of a day, eating delicacies not available in the forts, and gambling.

The extensive civilian settlement lay to the south and west of the fort, beneath the rich pasture. Aerial photography has revealed something of its plan – one can see a photograph in the Museum – but the visitor must go to Vindolanda to see what these settlements were like.

Those who are planning to visit the Willowford bridge abutment (page 40) ought to compare it with the similar remains at Chesters, but they will have to go back to Chollerford, cross the bridge, and take the footpath down the south bank of the river. It may be a tedious diversion, but it is well worth the effort. The Wall stands over eight feet high in places – an unusually narrow Wall on a broad foundation – terminating in a large tower, twenty-two feet square. The massive stones of the abutment have lewis-holes and grooves for tying rods, and a phallus, the symbol of good luck and fertility, is carved on the southern face. The mill-race is very clear, and so too are the signs of reconstruction on a larger scale.

From Chesters, the road winds up the hill towards Limestone Corner. On the right will be seen a good stretch of Wall, with turret 29a, now being conserved by the Department of the Environment after standing for nearly a hundred years without protection. At the summit there is a spectacular section of Wall ditch, and if possible the visitor should park in the small lay-by a hundred yards further on in order to inspect it. The soldiers have manfully slogged their way through solid rock, leaving some great slabs in the ditch, with the cramp holes ready to lift them out. But they never completed the task – perhaps some humane officer was prepared to sacrifice military efficiency in the face of common sense.

Between Limestone Corner and Carrawburgh – and indeed beyond – the Vallum stands out very clearly on the left of the road.

CARRAWBURGH (BROCOLITIA)

Admission: Always open and no charge. No *Museum* or *Custodian.*

Car-park: Alongside the fort.

Area of fort: 3½ acres. *Area of town:* Unknown.

Garrison: In the second century, the first cohort of Aquitanians and later the first cohort of Cugernians. In the third and fourth centuries the first cohort of Batavians.

Visible remains: Temple to Mithras.

This is one of the least inspiring fort sites, occupying a particularly dull stretch of moorland. The fort has been badly robbed by the builders of the Military Road, and there is nothing of interest to see today inside the ramparts. The fort is privately owned, but the Mithraeum has been placed in the guardianship of the Department of the Environment, who maintain a fenced-off footpath to it.

Outside the south-west corner of the fort, in a boggy stretch of ground, lie the remains of the most impressive temple to Mithras found in this country. The severe drought of 1949 caused the bog to shrink, and a visitor observed the tops of the three altars protruding through the surface of the marsh grass. The temple was completely excavated under the late Sir Ian Richmond's leadership in 1950. The building was constructed early in the third century and altered several times before it fell out of use in the fourth century, to be later sacked and destroyed, perhaps by Christians.

The door leads into an ante-chapel, where meals were prepared and ordeals took place. A wickerwork screen and door separated this chamber from the nave, with its raised benches on either side for worshippers. At the far end lay the sanctuary, with its altars dedicated by commanding officers from the fort: behind them there would have been a relief depicting Mithras slaying the bull. The altars and statues are now in the Museum of Antiquities at Newcastle University, where the reconstruction of the Mithraeum is the outstanding display of a very good Museum, but these replicas are realistic.

North-west of the Mithraeum, crossed by the field boundary, there is a small fenced off spring, usually covered with long grass and reeds. Here, in 1876, there was excavated the richest haul of Roman altars and coins ever found on the frontier: the water-tank belonged to a temple to the Celtic deity, Coventina, and worshippers had thrown into the water offerings of coins and other trinkets, but during some period of strife the contents of the temple had been thrown into the tank as well – over 13,000 coins were recovered, besides the many altars to Coventina now to be seen in Chesters Museum. The haul might have been greater but for the fact that week-end visitors made off with many of the finds. It is sad that this proud shrine should now be so neglected.

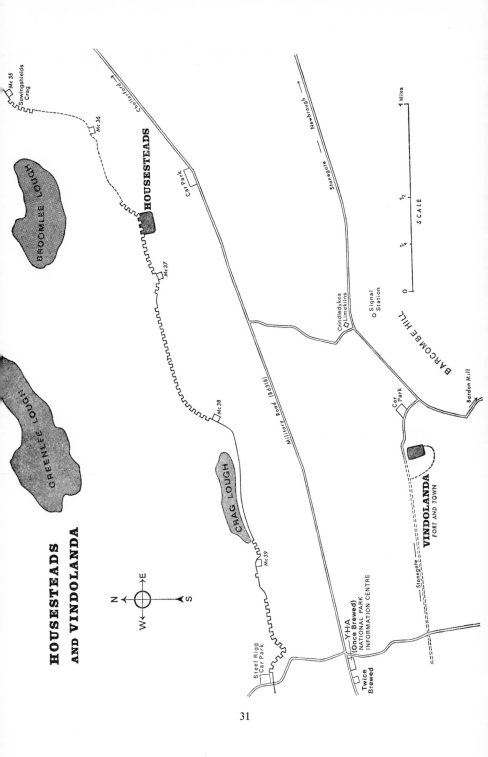

HOUSESTEADS
AND VINDOLANDA

Mc 35
Swingshields Crag

Mc 36

BROOMLEE LOUGH

HOUSESTEADS

Clayton Road

Car Park

Mc 37

GREENLEE LOUGH

Mc 38

CRAG LOUGH

Mc 39

Military Road (B.6318)

Steel Rigg
Car Park

Y.H.A
(Once Brewed)
NATIONAL PARK
INFORMATION CENTRE

Twice
Brewed

Newbrough

Stanegate

Crindledykes
Limekilns

o Signal
Station

BARCOMBE HILL

Bardon Mill

Car Park

VINDOLANDA
FORT AND TOWN

Stanegate

N
W ← ⊕ → E
S

SCALE

0   ¼   ½   1 Miles

31

7/15/72

HOUSESTEADS (VERCOVICIUM)

		Weekdays	Sundays
Opening hours	March – April	9.30 – 5.30	2.00 – 5.30
	May – Sept.	9.30 – 7.00	9.30 – 7.00
	October	9.30 – 5.30	2.00 – 5.30
	Nov. – Feb.	9.30 – 4.00	2.00 – 5.30

Admission: Adults 7½p; Children (under 15) 4p.
Reduced rates for parties.

Owned by the National Trust – remains in the guardianship of the Department of the Environment.

Car-park by the main road. 500 yards walk to the remains. *Museum.*

Guide-book by Eric Birley, other literature, slides, postcards, etc.

Excavations and conservation in progress, the former only for a few weeks in September.

Area of fort: 5 acres. *Area of town:* At least 10 acres.

Garrison: Second century: unknown. Third and fourth centuries: First cohort of Tungrians, reinforced at times by irregular units.

Visible remains: Some civilian houses outside the fort, all fort walls, gates and interval towers, latrine block, water-tanks, two barrack buildings, two granaries, headquarters building, commanding officer's residence, and part of the hospital. Good stretches of the Wall on both sides of the fort, together with the additional gateway (Knag Burn) to the east.

Housesteads has been the principal attraction on Hadrian's Wall since the eighteenth century: its remains are well preserved and its position on the Whin Sill ridge overlooking some of the most beautiful and remote Northumbrian countryside captures the spirit of the Roman frontier. Two fine walks along the Whin Sill start from here (to Steel Rigg and to Sewingshields). Understandably, the site is often crowded, and the wise visitor will arrive before 11 a.m. or after tea.

(NOTE: *The place is sometimes known as BORCOVICUS – a nineteenth century misnomer.*)

Before leaving the car park, look north towards the fort. The hillside is scarred by the cultivation terraces and streets of the civilian settlement: shops, inns, houses, temples and workshops cover around 10 acres, stretching from the fort walls on the south down to the bottom of the valley. Other civilian buildings shelter behind the eastern wall. The additional gateway through the Wall, to the east of the fort (Knag Burn) suggests that Housesteads may have been a substantial market-town frequented by those who lived beyond the Wall: when the garrison was at full strength (1,000 men), the population of the town must have reached 2,000 and more.

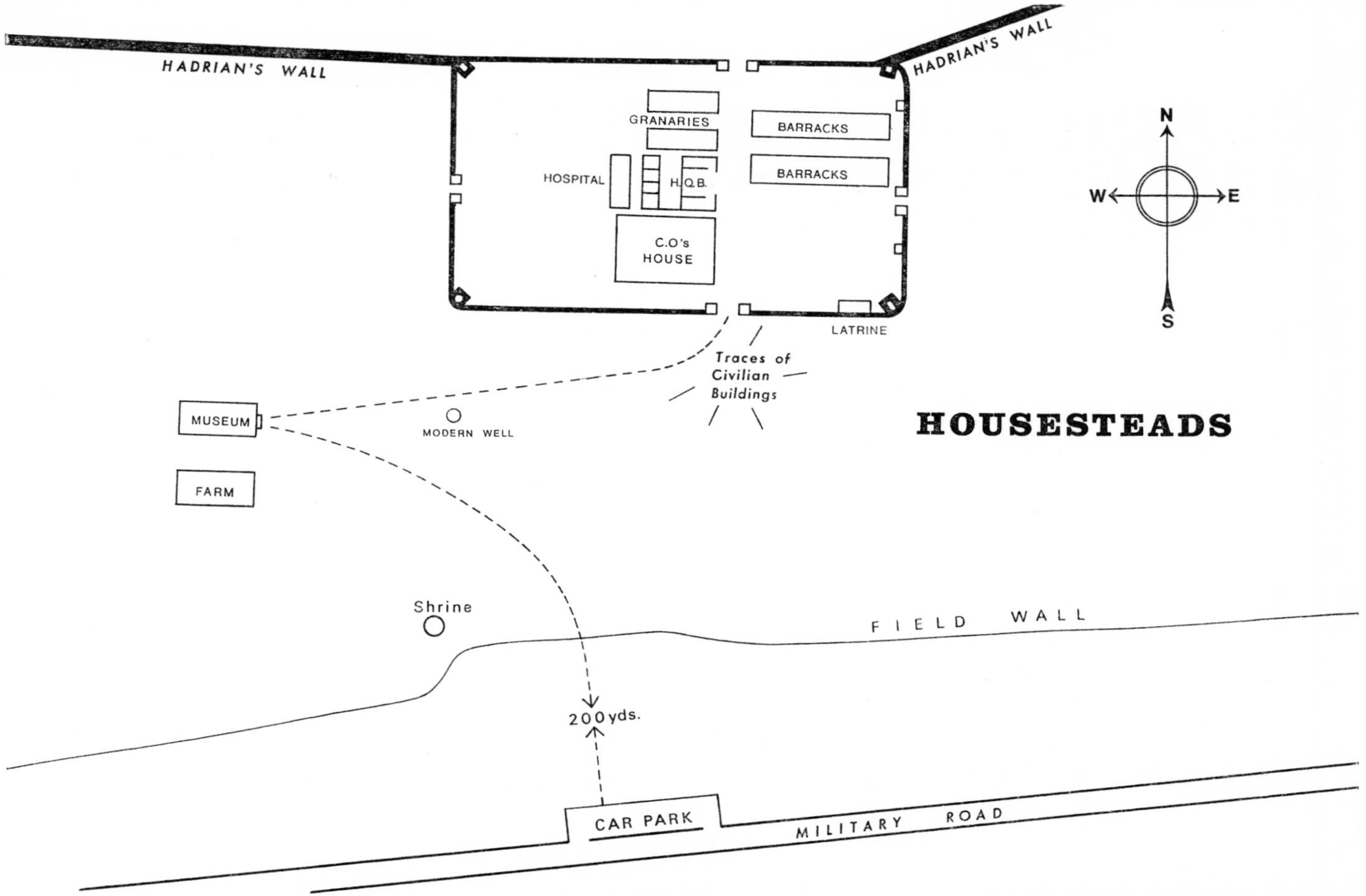

HOUSESTEADS

HADRIAN'S WALL

HADRIAN'S WALL

BARRACKS

BARRACKS

GRANARIES

H.Q.B.

HOSPITAL

C.O's HOUSE

LATRINE

Traces of Civilian Buildings

MODERN WELL

MUSEUM

FARM

Shrine

200 yds.

CAR PARK

FIELD WALL

MILITARY ROAD

N

E

S

W

After leaving the car-park, walk down the track (often muddy) and through the small iron gate at the foot of the main slope. To the left, surrounded by a dilapidated iron rail, there is a small shrine with a spring: today it provides the water for the farm house near the Museum, but it was once a Roman shrine. Excavation in 1961 recovered coins and other rubbish from the shallow tank, including a coin mould which some counterfeiter had used for making his own supplies. There must have been a temple compound here, for a Mithraeum, similar to that at Carrawburgh, was excavated many years ago, and a circular temple to Mars Thincsus lay within ten yards of the water-tank. Neither of these temples can be seen now.

Half way up the hill, bear slightly left for the Museum and Custodian's Office. Many years ago Housesteads was famed for its fierce Northumbrian Custodian, Mr. Thomas Thompson – a large bearded figure who dealt harshly with the frivolous visitor – but the present incumbents are more genial. Housesteads fort and Museum belong to the National Trust, having been presented to the nation by Mr. J. M. Clayton, but they are now in the guardianship of the Department of the Environment. The Museum, opened in 1936, was constructed entirely with fallen Roman stones recovered during excavations, and it was designed to be the same size as one of the civilian houses outside the fort walls. It is rather a dull and gloomy place, with fewer objects on view than the importance of the place warrants. It is, however, a merciful refuge during the heavy showers which frequently bombard this area. The most instructive exhibits are the models by William Bulmer of the fort and of a civilian house: one wishes they were four times larger. Two or three battered altars evoke most strongly the atmosphere of another age.

From the Museum, walk eastwards for a hundred yards or so, past the circular wall of a modern well, to the south gate of the fort, distorted by an old tower formerly an Armstrong haunt and by a Department of the Environment work-hut. A glance at the grass-covered road leading north into the heart of the fort will remind one that wheeled traffic would not attempt the gradient, and it is best to bear right and follow the southern wall to the impressive latrine block, the finest example of such a structure in Britain. Timber seating once covered the deep sewer channels on either side of the central platform, with its stone gutter and basins – where Roman soldiers would clean their sponges, a refined ancient custom in the absence of toilet paper. The sewer was flushed by water from the adjoining tanks, and the effluent was drained down the hillside. The building is not large for a garrison of 1,000 men, but each barrack building must have had toilet receptacles: this main latrine would, however, accommodate more than a dozen men at a time.

The near-by water tanks with their channels remind us that water was a precious commodity at this fort: there are no springs here, and the supply was maintained by collecting as much rain water as possible from the eaves of buildings to augment that pumped up from the Knag Burn, down the slope to the east.

Following the fort wall as it swings to the north, one reaches the East Gate, the principal entrance to the fort, whose Headquarters Building faces it. Its southern portal was blocked at some time, but the wheel ruts in the north portal – 4 ft. 8½ ins. apart – demonstrate that some Roman carts had the same wheel gauge as British Rail coaches. When John Hodgson excavated the southern guard chamber in 1833 he found a cartload of good coal stacked in a corner.

Housesteads East Gateway, north portal.

Continue north to see the badly planned junction of fort wall and great Wall before looking at the massive foundations of the north gate. It is worth passing through the field gate to see them from the north. The roadway has been cut away by Clayton's excavators to allow the impressive masonry to be seen.

At this point the buildings of the central range can be conveniently inspected. The two large granaries come first. Although not as inspiring as the Corstopitum examples, they show clearly the underfloor ventilation necessary in a building which housed not only the regimental corn supplies but also dried meat, fish, olive oil, lard, wine and beer, besides various luxury items such as fish sauces. The broad loading and service doors allowed carts to back up flush with the floor inside, and from here the individual centurions would draw their daily rations from a quartermaster. The southern granary has a later corn-drying kiln built into it.

To the south of the granaries, in the centre of the fort, lay the Headquarters Building. This was the administrative heart of the fort, containing the offices of the adjutant, the standard bearers and their clerks, the regimental Chapel of the Standards, the strong room for pay and savings, and the armouries. Unfortunately, the building has been severely robbed after late Roman alterations had already distorted the original plan. It does not compare with the much better examples of such buildings at Chesters and Vindolanda, but there is something to awake the imagination of all in the fragments of columns and pillar bases lying here, so remote from the heart of the Roman Empire.

To the south of the Headquarters lies the large courtyard house of the Commanding Officer, recently re-excavated by Miss Dorothy Charlesworth and others for the Department of the Environment. Alterations and re-constructions have blurred the plan, but the scale of the building is quite apparent, a reminder that the commanding officer expected his army residence to be on the same scale as his private house nearer Italy: he would hope to have his family with him, together with servants and slaves. The excavation of his private latrine revealed a gold finger ring trapped in a sewer crack.

Immediately to the west of the Headquarters lay the fort Hospital, now in the process of re-excavation. There is little intelligible to see at the moment, but it is a reminder that the Roman army medical service was a well developed and essential part of the soldiers' lives. This building had a series of wards, stores and operating theatres surrounded a spacious courtyard. Only the larger forts possessed these facilities.

At this point the visitor should walk westwards to see the fourth Gate – well preserved, although both portals were ultimately blocked during the Roman occupation. The entire western portion of the fort was occupied by barrack buildings, although none are visible now. The two excavated examples in the eastern range are fragmentary – those at Chesters give a much clearer impression of a Roman soldier's accommodation.

Having seen the fort, it is worth walking back to the East Gate and descend the slope to the Knag Burn, the small stream which rises to the north of the Wall and flows under it in a culvert. A hundred yards or so from the Wall, downstream, lie the mounds which cover the military bath-house. Traces of walling can be seen amongst the nettles. On the Wall itself, just east of the Burn, lie the remains of the special gateway through the Wall, with guard chambers. Here travellers could be searched, or taxed, or both.

See pages 53 and 54 for the walks from Housesteads to Sewingshields Crag and Housesteads to Steel Rigg.

VINDOLANDA (Chesterholm)

Opening hours	April	9.30 – 5.00
	May – Sept.	9.30 – 6.30
	Oct. – March	10.30 – 3.30
Admission:	Adults 10p; Pensioners 5p;	
	Children (under 18) 2½p.	

Car-park on the approach road, 400 yards east of the site.
Museum.
Guide book by Robin Birley, other literature, replicas, posters, postcards, soft drinks, etc.
Excavation and conservation in progress throughout the year.
Area of fort: 3 acres; *Area of town:* approximately 10 acres.
  Garrison (third and fourth centuries): Fourth Cohort of Gauls, part-mounted.

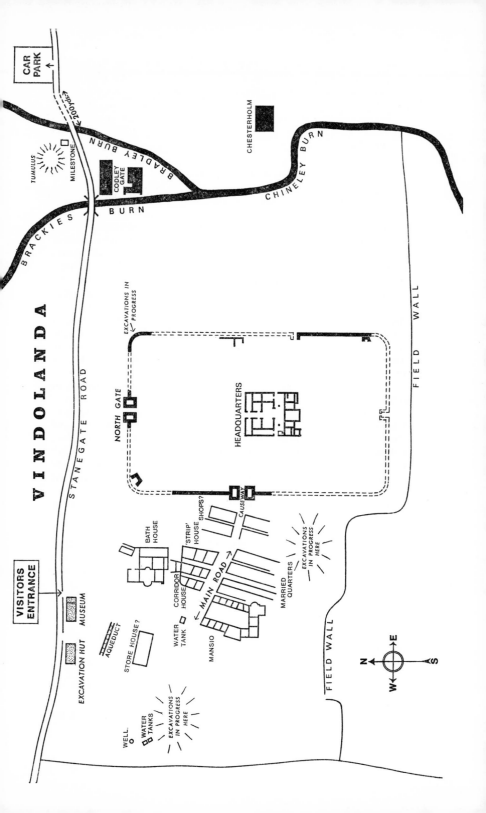

Visible remains: Roman milestone in position on Stanegate, three fort gates, stretches of fort wall, two ballista platforms, headquarters building, flagged roadway from fort to town, military bath-house, *mansio* or inn for travellers, corridor house, shops, domestic houses, water-tanks and a well. As large scale excavation is in progress, many other buildings may be visible.

Vindolanda lies two miles W.S.W. of Housesteads on the Stanegate. The best route is to turn off the Military Road half a mile west of the Housesteads car-park and follow the direction signs.

This is a very unusual site: in 1970 it was presented by its owner to an archaeological Trust, a registered charity, whose declared intention it is to excavate and have conserved the entire remains. A full-time staff are employed, and the Trust's funds come from private donations and subscriptions, augmented by the admission fees and profits from sales. For much of the year courses in practical archaeology are run on the site, many of them taken up by school parties from the northern education authorities. If the Trust are able to complete their programme, this will be far and away the largest visible Roman site in Britain. The remains of the fort were placed in the guardianship of the Department of the Environment by Eric Birley, a former owner, but the Vindolanda Trust is responsible for the conservation of masonry exposed in the town.

Some visitors find Chesters and Housesteads rather dead sites – they have the look of a well tended private garden – but Vindolanda is very different. Excavation on a large scale involves major earth-moving problems, and here the inevitable spoil-heaps and excavation equipment add a new dimension to the remains. Visitors will find that they can legitimately view the excavation work from close quarters, but they must respect the wire fences which separate them from areas whose examination is not yet completed. Saturdays are usually the excavators' days off.

The *Museum*, a temporary structure, houses material discovered in the *vicus* or small town in the past three years. Particularly important are the items of female adornment found in the drains of the military bath-house, but the whole display emphasises that the civilians on the Wall possessed a standard of living little different from that of the troops. Most of the fine altars discovered here in the past are now on display in Chesters Museum.

After leaving the Museum, visitors should view the remains of the bath-house, whose western walls stand nearly eight feet high. It will be some time before it is possible to look closely at the building, for the badly burned stones require detailed treatment which will take a year or two. The semi-circular wall at the western end contained the hot-plunge bath, and the blackened hypocaust pillars to the south once lay beneath the floor of the warm room. Two hundred and seventy years ago the roof of the room was still in place.

From the bath-house, continue south to the main road through the town – excavated roads here have a thin layer of red gravel on their surface, to distinguish them from the other gravel on the floors of buildings. South of the road lies the large *mansio* or inn for travellers. Such buildings were to be found every twenty miles or so along the main roads throughout the Roman Empire, but this is the only example to be seen in Britain. The large courtyard was open to the skies, and the first three rooms on each side were small guest rooms. Beyond them lay a latrine, kitchen and dining room, with a small suite of baths at the southern end. The huge blocks of stone on the eastern wall were placed there in the reconstruction of A.D. 300 by men who had no faith in the conventional building methods of old.

The gold ring featuring Medusa was found upon the latrine floor.

On the other side of the main road lies the corridor-house, with three rooms on either side of a central passageway. This was probably the home of a retired soldier, or perhaps a merchant. The left-hand front room has triple drains in its floor, suggesting use as a butcher's shop, whilst the right hand rear room has a small latrine. Both the military standard and the Anima Mea gold ring came from this building.

To the east of the corridor house lies a normal domestic house of the kind usually called 'strip houses'. This would be the home of perhaps an N.C.O. – the private soldiers' families were more likely to occupy a single room of the large married quarters blocks (currently being excavated on the other side of the road). The roadway from here into the fort is particularly impressive: it was constructed in A.D. 300, when a new fort (that now visible) was constructed.

Inside the fort, the west and north gateways alone possessed guard chambers, and they are on a reduced scale from those of the more ambitious forts on the Wall. The Headquarters Building in the centre of the fort is exceptionally well preserved. At the southern end lie the administrative rooms: those on the eastern side were occupied by the standard bearers, on the western side by the adjutant and his clerks. The Chapel of the Standards, in the centre, has an unusual sunken pit behind it for the pay and savings. On the western side, in the large cross-hall, are the remains of the commanding officer's tribunal or rostrum, from which he could address his troops, fallen in under cover. The well in the courtyard was eighteen feet deep, sunk down to bedrock. It produced a variety of wooden and leather objects, including a cabbage stalk.

It is worth walking to the north-east angle of the fort, to see the recently excavated section of fort wall, and to view the surrounding countryside. The dominant feature is Barcombe hill, clad in heather and bracken: on its southern end one can see the quarry faces, one of which still bears the marks of Roman masons. At the northern end of the hill there is a Roman signal station, inserted into the ruins of a native fort. Two lengths of Hadrian's Wall are visible from here – that above Hot Bank farm to the north-east, and Winshields summit to the north-east. The views to the south are extensive. Some visitors wonder why a fort should have been placed here rather than on the summit of Barcombe, and it should be remembered that the Romans were not primarily concerned with defensive positions – a well drained plateau and a good water supply were much more important.

Vindolanda had a longer life than Chesters or Housesteads, for it was originally one of the Stanegate frontier forts, like Corbridge, and it will need constant excavation for very many years before its full history can be examined. In most parts of the field, there are the superimposed remains of at least four different structures.

If the milestone has not been examined on the way up to the fort, it should be visited on the return journey, for it is the only one remaining of all the Roman milestones which still stands to its full height in its original position. It once carried an inscription, but no lettering can be seen on it now.

WILLOWFORD BRIDGE ABUTMENT

Opening hours: Daylight.
No car-park, Museum or Custodian.
Admission charges: Adults 5p; Children 2½p; Bus parties 100p.
Visible remains: A fine stretch of narrow wall built on broad wall foundation, two turrets (48 a and b) and exceptionally massive foundations of the bridge abutment, together with guard tower. Wall ditch to north is followed by the modern farm-track.

Approaching from the east, turn left in Gilsland village and stop near the school, by a Department of the Environment signpost to the bridge. There is no car-park down the farm track, and vehicles should be left on the verge. Pay admission charge at the farm house close to the bridge.

It is well worth giving up an hour or so to the inspection of this fine stretch of Wall. The remains of the turrets show clearly how they were constructed with broad wing walls, before the change of plan resulted in the construction of the narrow Wall between them. A good couple of hundred yards of Wall ditch, with the modern farm track running inside it, heightens the effect of the Wall. From the farm-house, where the admission fee should be paid, one can see Harrow's Scar milecastle on the top of the escarpment across the river. Birdoswald fort lies just behind the milecastle.

The Stanegate and Wall fort of Vindolanda, under a light covering of snow in December 1967. The prominent playing-card shape of the fourth-century fort is clearly visible, and the *vicus* or small frontier town lies beyond. Much of the *vicus* has now been excavated.

Photograph by J. K. St. Joseph, copyright Cambridge University Dept. of Aerial Photography.

The Roman milestone opposite Codley Gate farm on the Stanegate, below the fort of Vindolanda. A tumulus lies close by. This is the only milestone still standing to its full height in its original position in Britain. The stump of the next stone to the west can still be seen, just over one Roman mile (1618 yards) away.

7/17/72 Part of the huge complex at Corbridge, known as site XI. Such large masonry is exceptional, and points to some special function for the building.

Small bronze cockerel, from a civilian house.

Roman military standard in bronze.

Betrothal medallion in Whitby jet.

Some recent finds from Vindolanda.

Birdoswald: S. gateway (*porta decumana*)

(John Storey, 1850)

The Wall to the east of Cawfields milecastle, winding along the crest of the crags. There was no necessity for a ditch to the north of the Wall in such stretches.

Abutment of Roman bridge opposite Chester's Bath-house. At Willowford,
near Birdoswald, there are equally impressive remains of the Roman bridge
across the Irthing.
Lithograph

Birdoswald, western rampart. Judging by the comments of excavators the remains of this fort are very well preserved below the turf.

Old Print after painting by H. B. Richardson

(a) This altar was found in the *vicus* or frontier town outside the fort at Vindolanda, and records a dedication to VULCAN, God of metal workers, by the 'vicani Vindolandesses', the civilians of Vindolanda.

(b) Altar to Jupiter, set up by a Commanding Officer of the Fourth Cohort of Gauls, Quintus Petronius Urbicus.

Both altars are now in Chesters Museum.

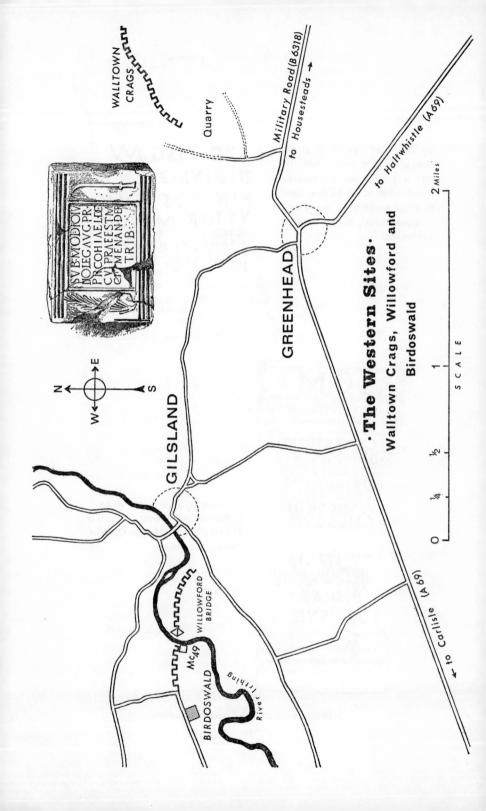

The Western Sites.
Walltown Crags, Willowford and Birdoswald

WALLTOWN CRAGS

Quarry

Military Road (B 6318)

to Housesteads →

to Haltwhistle (A69)

GREENHEAD

← to Carlisle (A69)

SCALE

0   ¼   ½   1   2 Miles

GILSLAND

N
W —●— E
S

WILLOWFORD BRIDGE

Mc 49

BIRDOSWALD

River Irthing

SVBMODIOV
NOIEGAVGPR
PRCOHIAELC
CVPRAEESTM
MENANDE
TRIB

Follow the Wall down into the valley, a natural amphitheatre, surrounded by wooded banks. Much of the Wall is standing five or six feet high, with a rubble core containing much washed stone from the river bed. The Irthing has changed course since Roman days, eroding the western bank and leaving the piers of the old bridge beneath the green meadow.

The massive eastern bridge abutment, with guard tower, has been comprehensively reconstructed in Roman days, but the remains of its mill race are quite clear. The Wall had to be carried across three major rivers – (the North Tyne, the Eden and the Irthing here), besides a number of substantial streams, requiring advanced engineering skills.

It is worth pausing to look back at the Wall to the east of Willowford, and appreciate the enormous quantities not only of cut stone but also rubble core, lime and water that were necessary even for a small stretch. The two foot reduction in width, from 10 Roman feet to eight, made a substantial difference, but one would have thought that even eight feet was unnecessarily broad.

BIRDOSWALD TO HARROW'S SCAR MILECASTLE

Having seen Willowford bridge, it is necessary to drive back through Gilsland, bearing left to cross the bridge and left again soon afterward, ignoring the tempting signpost 'Moscow 1¼ m'. The first left after this takes one up to Birdoswald. The car should be left in the lay-by near the Wall. It is a short walk eastward, by a high stretch of Wall, to the remains of Harrow's Scar milecastle (49). The old Turf Wall milecastle which preceded it was located beneath the present structure in 1953. The view from here can be magnificent.

BIRDOSWALD (CAMBOGLANNA)

Opening hours: Hours of daylight.

Admission (pay at the farm-house): Adults 5p, children 2½p.

No Museum or car-park.

Guide-book by Peter Howard.

Area of fort: Over 5 acres.   *Area of town:* Unknown.

Garrison: Designed for a cavalry regiment, but soon occupied by infantry, 1,000 strong. Third and fourth century Hadrian's first cohort of Dacians, 1,000 strong.

Visible remains: Stretches of fort walls and junctions with Hadrian's Wall, interval and angle towers and gates.

Birdoswald lies on a level plateau high above the Irthing, perhaps the most inspiring of all sites on the Wall. It has claims to be the Camelot of Arthur. The few visible remains, all part of the defences, are well enough preserved to whet the appetite for more excavation and conservation. Work in the past has revealed that the southern wall of the Headquarters is still standing fifteen courses high beneath the turf, and the building to the west of it was nearly eight feet high. It was at Birdoswald between 1927 and 1933 that so much of our knowledge of the Wall's various structural periods was worked out: the Turf Wall originally joined the fort on both sides well to the south of its later replacement in stone, so that the fort was intended to hold a cavalry regiment when first built.

The visitor who has already seen the remains of the other forts will find the main East Gate very rewarding: it stands higher than any other on the Wall today. Apart from this gate, however, there is little of interest to see in the fort, but the view should be appreciated by walking to the edge of the bank, to the south of the fort.

WALKS ALONG THE LINE OF THE WALL

Four of the finest sections of Wall are described on the following pages: three of them conveniently start or finish close to pubs. Those with the inclination will therefore time their walk carefully. The approximate length of time the walk will take is indicated, taking into account some leisurely exploration and photographic activity. Those who have access to two cars will save themselves a tedious return journey if they park a car at the finishing point before commencing. Public transport along the military road is rare, and private cars are usually more concerned with speed than with giving people lifts. If you do have a walk along part of this road, take great care.

Many people have discovered that a walk along the Wall does not have to take place on a summer's afternoon: under snow it can be an exhilarating experience, with some of the thrills of a ridge walk usually reserved to higher hills. It can also be a wonderful experience making the journey in the late evening, with glorious sunsets and sometimes a much closer contact with the spirit of the frontier. One thing is quite certain: one must walk the Wall in order to appreciate the magnitude of the engineering feat, and to enjoy the superb scenery.

HOUSESTEADS TO SEWINGSHIELDS CRAG
AND RETURN

Time: 1 hour 45 minutes.

This is an excellent walk for visitors who have completed their inspection of Housesteads and wish to taste the atmosphere of one of the most exposed and uninhabited parts of the Whin Sill. If one starts at the north-east angle of the fort, one can inspect the Knag Burn gateway across the small stream which flows beneath the Wall in a culvert. Just to the south, down the slope, there is a Roman well and the grass covered mounds which conceal the military bath-house. Water was pumped from here up to the fort.

Once the wood has been entered, the Wall is no longer visible until near the end of the walk, on the summit of Sewingshields Crag. Even the field wall now running on the foundations of the Wall is dilapidated, and the visitor can concentrate upon the magnificent views in all directions. To the west, Housesteads fort and the crags beyond are dramatic, and the views to the south of the wooded Allen valley and the moors beyond are rarely bettered. To the north and north-west, Broomlee Lough and crags have a wild backcloth of moors and forests.

Arthurian legends are very strong here, for a shepherd is supposed to have stumbled across the entrance to a cave where the King and his Court still sleep, awaiting a call from the spell-dissolving horn which lay near-by. The old castle of Sewingshields has been demolished: it was once a border stronghold of men who cared little for the King's writ. Broomlee Lough conceals the treasure of a former baron of Sewingshields. Visitors should refer to Richardson's Table Books to read full accounts of these legends.

From the summit of Sewingshields one can see the mysterious Black Dyke, a very old earthwork of some kind, running towards the Wall from the north: it has been traced from Tarset in the North Tyne valley to the South Tyne, but both its date and its purpose are unknown.

This region embodies the spirit of the old Border days as much as those of Roman occupation, and it is best appreciated on a wild and windy day.

HOUSESTEADS TO STEEL RIGG

Time: 1 hour 45 minutes.

This is the most frequented of all walks along the Wall, the scene of countless photographs and a very beautiful route, but it does not compare with the Walltown Crags to Cawfields section for instructive remains. The path is well defined throughout, and it is possible to walk along the Wall itself for much of the way (here the property of the National Trust and conserved in a different manner from the Department of the Environment sections).

Walkers should start from the north-west angle of Housesteads fort and follow the Wall through the thin fir plantation. The drop to the north is steep, allowing the Romans to forgo a ditch. Milecastle 37 (Housesteads milecastle) lies in the first dip, little more than 400 yards from the fort. The north gateway is particularly interesting, for the original ten-foot doorway in fine large masonry has been reduced by blocking walls to a narrow passage. The milecastle produced one of the inscriptions recording construction by the Second Legion under Platorius Nepos, Hadrian's governor of Britain.

Visitors will observe that although the north face of the Wall is a continuous line, there are differences in width which result in awkward joints on the inner (southern) face. This is presumably because the centurions in charge of construction gangs were following a line marked out for them on the north side, but had to use their own judgment as to the exact width of the Wall, with the rather scrappy results one can still see.

Beyond the milecastle, the Wall follows the undulations of the crags, and from the summit above Hot Bank farm it is worth a lengthy pause to take stock of the surrounding countryside. To the west, Crag Lough's water, now stocked with trout, laps the broken rocks at the foot of the crags, whilst Greenlee Lough and Broomlee Lough are visible to north and north-east. The gloomy wastes of Kielder forest, Europe's largest man-made wood, blot out the horizon. To the south-east Grindon Lough, in summer little more than a puddle, can be seen, and beyond that, across South Tyne, the moors rise up, with the heavily wooded Allen valley dividing them. To south-west the Pennine hills of Cross Fell and Cold Fell can be seen, and sometimes Skiddaw and Saddleback rising behind them.

Dropping down the bank, one passes the robbed out site of milecastle 38 before crossing the small stream and the farm track and entering the wood on the southern shore of Crag Lough. The Wall here has been demolished for a long stretch, but the exhilarating heights of the Whin Sill compensate. This is a favourite haunt of rock-climbers: although the cliffs are not high, the rock is good and the climbs are hard enough to test both learners and the experienced. The temptation to throw a stone into the Lough must be avoided, since climbers are often below, preparing their equipment.

Beyond Crag Lough, Castle Nick milecastle (39) lies in a convenient hollow, before the Wall rises once more. Steel Rigg car park, amongst the trees, should now be in sight, as will be the conveniently placed Youth Hostel (Once Brewed), the National Park Information Centre and the pub (Twice Brewed). This is a good place for refreshments before deciding upon the next stage.

STEEL RIGG TO CAWFIELDS

Time: 1 hour 45 minutes.

Transport can be left in the Steel Rigg car-park amongst the trees – with its award winning toilets – before crossing the stile south of the entrance. Cows tend to shelter near the Wall in bad weather, which can make the going somewhat treacherous to the person whose eyes are elsewhere. The trig point on the top of the hill marks the highest point on the Wall, 1,230 feet above sea level, and the views can be tremendous. To the north-east the border line and Cheviot are visible, with both Greenlee and Crag Lough in the foreground. The Wall ditch running down the bank to Steel Rigg is as well preserved here as anywhere. To the west the Solway can be seen on a clear day, with the towers of Spadeadam rocket range further north.

For much of the way the Wall cannot be inspected, although the field wall running above it contains a mass of Roman stone. Below the crags to the north the swampy fields present their own formidable obstacle. Keen eyes may detect the positions of mile-castles 40 and 41, but for much of the way it is best to concentrate upon the scenery as one passes up and down the crests – from Bogle Hole Gap to Caw Gap and Bloody Gap. Quite suddenly a fine piece of Wall, 13 courses high, appears in Thorny Doors, and from there to Cawfields milecastle the quality of the Department of the Environment's conservation efforts can be appreciated. To the south, the Vallum is clearly seen, with traces of the Roman military way close to it. North of the Wall, down below the cliffs, there are a surprising number of small farmhouses scattered about in the last open countryside before Kielder forest.

Cawfields milecastle (42) should be inspected carefully. Both north and south gates exhibit massive masonry, with the door holes still in position. The Walls are eight feet thick. The small barrack buildings inside the milecastle must have rested uncomfortably on the considerable slope.

Beyond the milecastle, Cawfields quarry has removed a great slice of Wall, and further destruction was prevented by the payment of compensation to landowners. At this point one can take the road down to the inn nearby.

WALLTOWN CRAGS TO CAWFIELDS QUARRY

Time: 2 hours.

Spectacular stretches of Wall conserved by the Department of the Environment, remains of turrets and milecastles, evidence of massive destruction by modern quarries, untreated and unexcavated portions of Wall, Greatchesters Fort.

It is best to walk this very fine stretch from west to east for two good reasons: the prevailing wind is normally behind one, and the rather dull last mile is enlivened by the proximity of the Milecastle Inn on the Military Road, where first-class bar meals can be consumed with the necessary beverages. The visitor then has time to take stock and decide upon the next stage.

Although this is not the most popular walk along the Wall, many regard it as being by far the most instructive and enjoyable. Within a few yards one can see those magnificent stretches of Wall above Walltown Crags which have been carefully conserved by the Department of the Environment, yet observe also the ghostly moonscapes of the large quarries which have removed both Wall and Whin Sill, the dilapidated stretches as yet unexcavated and untreated, the wonderful views to the north of untamed moorland and waste, the odious electricity pylons to the south, and finally, but perhaps most instructive of all, the sad dereliction at the fort of Greatchesters. Here the lesson of man's preservation of his heritage is driven home most forcefully: it costs a great deal of money to make excavated buildings safe and to display them for the benefit of visitors, but it is a price worth paying.

56

Visitors should turn off the Military Road above Greenhead village. There are no car-parks, and it is best to leave the car on the broad verges near the quarry (where a notice bars buses from proceeding any further).* Take the narrow road to the right, to the south of the quarry, and follow it to the cattle-grid. Then follow the field wall on the left to the summit of the ridge, some 300 yards, and find the Wall in front of one, sawn off to the west by the destruction of twentieth-century man. The whinstone quarry on the left is a spectacular sight: further damage to the Wall was prevented by Government compensation to halt the advance. The fine views to the west are spoiled by the massed series of electricity pylons.

Walking to the east, the Wall is in very good condition and close inspection of the first few hundred yards will reveal much information about its construction. A great deal of the core is whinstone, and some facing stones have been cut from the same hard rock. There is an unusual corbelled corner, where the Wall has to change direction on a steep slope, and for a few yards it runs on the north of the actual crest; some large whin boulders have been incorporated into its foundations. Near the first summit it should be possible to find a centurial stone built into the north face of the Wall upside down, on the second lowest course (close to the Department of the Environment notice on the south side announcing the fact that this is Walltown Crags). The stone, on which 'COH III' is clear, has found its way into this position during reconstruction of the Wall, for such stones are normally confined to the southern face. In the wood below, on the north side, chives and other rare herbs can be found which some believe were introduced to this country by Roman soldiers who needed them for medicinal purposes.

This summit is one of the Nine Nicks of Thirlwall which the Wall bestrides effortlessly. The various manoeuvres which it adopts in the gaps between the Nicks – and the positioning of short stretches of ditch on the north side – must have been worked out with great satisfaction by Roman staff officers obsessed with a theory of defence which the Wall was not constructed to deal with. There are several good examples which show how the courses of stone remained horizontal when the Wall climbed a steep slope, reminding us that the rampart walk must also have been stepped at these points.

As one reaches the end of the conserved section, before the old quarry which has removed a quarter of a mile of Wall, a turret is visible (45a). It was built before the Wall as a free-standing signalling station, similar to that on Pike Hill to the west of Birdoswald, and the Wall was later joined to it.

*NOTE: Carvoran fort lies to the left of the quarry, but there is nothing for the visitor to see at the moment.

Size, 3 feet 8 inches by 1 foot 11 inches.

Tombstone of an archer, found at Housesteads. It is one of the minor mysteries of the Wall, for the only recorded regiment of archers were based at Carvoran.

Tombstone from Chesters of Aurelius Victor, aged 50. The Roman habit of recording the age of the deceased enables us to estimate average life expectancy.

Size, 4 feet by 2 feet 6 inches.

Beyond the chasm left by the quarry, there are the remains of a milecastle (45), before one crosses the broad gap and climbs up the next Nick, where a fine turret stands uneasily two thirds of the way up the bank. This was excavated in 1892 and stands nine courses high (44b). It is in need of conservation. Five yards from its southern wall lie the three stones from its arched doorway.

From here onwards the remains of the Wall are visible, but the contrast between this stretch and that preserved by the Department of the Environment is very marked. One can only hope that the whole stretch will one day be treated, before further destruction takes place.

Milecastle 44's robbed walls should be visible east of Allolee farm house, but by now the ruins of Greatchesters fort should be in sight. Field gates, along the line of the old military way, take one up to its north-west angle tower. Greatchesters fort occupies the half-way point on the original line of the Wall: a good deal of excavation has been carried out in the past, particularly in the 1890's, and the west tower of the south gate revealed an exceptional hoard of jewellery, but the contrast between the visible remains here and those at Housesteads or Vindolanda speaks for itself. The position of the fort is not dramatic and the overgrown and rotting structures cast a gloom over one's appreciation of the Wall. The West Gate, however, exhibits blocking walls which closed it completely in the fourth century, and the arch of the strong-room in the centre of the fort demonstrates how well some of the structures must be surviving beneath the grass. A large altar, with sculptured side panel, stands uneasily in the eastern chamber of the south gate.

Further comments about Greatchesters are superfluous, and by now the white building of the Milecastle Inn is visible on the Military Road. It is a short stretch from the fort to the road by Cawfields quarry: passing down the road there are the grass covered remains of Haltwhistle Burn fortlet on the right – a strange little site which belonged to the Stanegate system – or perhaps to the early years of the Wall, before the forts were added to it. It is best to pass by and get to the pub.

A POSSIBLE ITINERARY

You can see the Wall and something of its setting in a day, but this will not give you much more than a superficial acquaintance. The remains described in this guide need three days of your time to be appreciated properly, and the following time-table gives a rough guide to those who want to explore thoroughly.

First day

It is best to start at Corbridge. The remains are impressive and the Museum will introduce you to the considerable range of utensils and domestic goods that the soldiers and civilians possessed. The modern village is an attractive place, and its

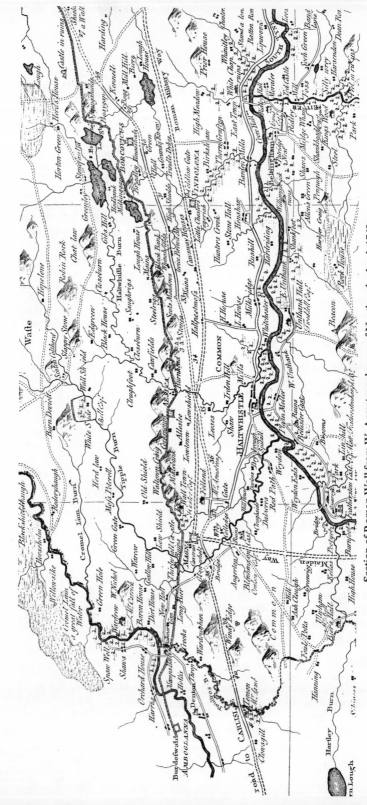

Section of Roman Wall from W. Armstrong's map of Northumberland, 1769.

Church is well worth inspecting. There are also antique shops, cafes and a good choice of pubs. If the visitor is not familiar with local customs and speech, he would do well to call at the Wheatsheaf Hotel, and take an early lunch.

From Corbridge, it is a quarter of an hour's journey by car, on the north side of the Tyne, by-passing Hexham, through Wall village and Chollerford to Chesters. This was perhaps the finest fort-site on the Wall, much more sheltered than most, on the north bank of a broad river (North Tyne). The Museum is crammed with fine altars, taken from several forts on the Wall.

After Chesters, climb the steep bank to the west, and enter the true Wall country, with long views of moorland and hills, and a minimum of modern buildings. With luck it should be possible to park in the lay-by just beyond Limestone Corner to see the Wall ditch and Vallum cuttings in the rock, before reaching the Carrawburgh car-park. The Mithraeum is the best preserved temple on the Wall, but there is little else to see. There should still be time on the first day for a walk along a stretch of Wall, and the Steel Rigg to Housesteads section is probably the best at this stage. Those who are wilting need not walk very far to appreciate the Wall's superb position on the crags.

Second day

The second day calls for two lengthy visits to the forts and civilian remains at Housesteads and Vindolanda. While at the former, the walk from the fort to Sewingshields crag is well worth while. At Vindolanda the visitor may wish to pause for a while to watch excavation in progress. Thereafter there should be time to walk from Steel Rigg car-park to Cawfields.

Third day

The third day leaves plenty of time for the finest walk of all, from Walltown Crags to Cawfields, before travelling west to see the fine remains at Willowford Bridge, together with Birdoswald and Harrow's Scar milecastle.

THE STANEGATE AND NEWBROUGH

If the visitor has been to Vindolanda or Housesteads and wants to return to Hexham by the most direct route, he should join the Stanegate near the old lime-kilns at Crindledykes, not far from Vindolanda. Here the modern road runs above the old Roman highway, past Grindon Lough on the left – the home of whooper swans in the winter, sometimes ninety strong – and on through the little village of Newbrough. The pleasant church of St. Peter Stonecroft stands on the site of another fort which belonged to the Stanegate series. It is seven miles from Vindolanda. The Red Lion is one of the better pubs in the area, well worth sampling. Beyond Newbrough, the road crosses the railway and joins the A69 a short distance west of Hexham.

Altar to the god Antenociticus, set up by a centurion of the Twentieth Legion. It was found in a small shrine outside the fort at Benwell.

The great majority of these altars belong to the second and early third centuries. Declining standards of literacy and the advent of Christianity led to their disappearance.

Acknowledgments for photographs
We wish to thank Turners Ltd. for the aerial photo of the Vallum and the Vindolanda Trust and Stanley Buck for the remaining photographs.

Hexham Abbey is one of the oldest stone-built churches in Britain, and it has the added attraction of numerous Roman stones in its fabric, mainly looted from Corbridge. The great tombstone of the standard bearer should be seen here. Another local church with impressive Roman material lies at Chollerton, not far from Chesters. Columns from that fort's headquarters building are still serving a useful function.

GENERAL INFORMATION

Many visitors to the Wall stay in Newcastle or Carlisle, but there are plenty of good hotels, boarding houses and bed and breakfast establishments within the central sector of the Wall. Hexham and Corbridge are perhaps the best bases, but those who have a caravan will find an excellent site at Yont the Cleugh, near Coanwood, south of Haltwhistle. The Once Brewed Youth Hostel on the Military Road west of Housesteads is justly famous as a centre for Wall studies. Camping sites are few and far between at the moment, but some farmers will let you put up a tent, on payment of a small fee. Those wanting an up-to-date list of bed and breakfast houses should call at the local Council offices in either Hexham or Haltwhistle.

The National Park Information Centre, next door to the Once Brewed Youth Hostel, will answer many of your questions.

Early closing days in Haltwhistle and Hexham are Wednesdays and Thursdays respectively.

BIBLIOGRAPHY

The majority of the standard reference works are now dated by research subsequent to their publication, but if the visitor bears this in mind the following works will help him towards a deeper understanding of the frontier:

Handbook to the Roman Wall, 12th ed., Bruce and Richmond (1966).

Research on Hadrian's Wall by Eric Birley (1961).

Ordnance Survey 2-inch map of the Wall.

Guide-books to Corbridge, Chesters and Housesteads by Eric Birley (H.M.S.O.).

Guide-book to Vindolanda by Robin Birley.

Guide-book to Birdoswald by Peter Heward.

The relevant chapters dealing with the frontier in both Richmond's *Roman Britain* (Penguin) and Frere's *Britannia* (Routledge and Kegan Paul) will help to set the Wall in its proper perspective.

Detailed references to other works will be found both in Birley, *Research on Hadrian's Wall*, and in the *Handbook*.

TYNESIDE ███████████████ Bio-
graphies of ██████████████ artists and
architects. Lavishly illustrated. £2.50

PICTURE PIONEERS by *G. Mellor*. The history
of the Movies in Northern England.
Illustrated. £1.50

NEWCASTLE PAST AND PRESENT by *D.
Dougan*. With outstanding illustrations. .. £2.00

THE LINDISFARNE STORY. A saga of Island
Folk by *C. Cromarty* 60p

WHAT THE BUTLER SAW IN
NORTHUMBRIA. A humorous guide to
the area by *William Butler*, director of
Northumbria Travel Association 60p

NORTHUMBERLAND & DURHAM,
INDUSTRY IN 19th CENTURY. 128
illustrations £2.50

THE SMELL OF SUNDAY DINNER by *Sid
Chaplin*. North Country Essays. Illustrated £1.50

TOMMY ARMSTRONG SINGS. Collection of
the Stanley pitman poet's songs. Illustrated 40p

BIRDS OF THE KIELDER by *W. McCavish* .. 50p

THE CONTRACTING COALFIELD. Maps
showing the rise and decline of the Durham
Coalfield by *W. Moyes* £2.50

THE BLACKPOOL STORY. A light hearted
history and guide to Blackpool by *Scott
Dobson* 25p

VIEWS ON THE MANCHESTER AND
LEEDS RAILWAY by *A. F. Tait*. 1845.
Facsimile. Folio Size.. .. .. .. £6.00

HISTORY OF BRITISH BIRDS by *Thomas
Bewick*. Facsimile. Two volumes. .. .. £3.50 each

THOMAS BEWICK, HIS LIFE AND TIMES
by *Robert Robinson*. 1887. Facsimile. 200
Illustrations. £4.00

THOSE DELAVALS by *Roger Burgess*. Based on
BBC Television story.. .. .. .. 55p